This journal belongs to

....

Published in the UK by Scholastic Children's Books, 2020
Euston House, 24 Eversholt Street, London, NW1 1DB
A division of Scholastic Limited

London – New York – Toronto – Sydney - Auckland
Mexico City – New Delhi – Hong Kong

Adapted from *Smart Girl's Guide to Life*
Original text by Sally Morgan

ISBN 978-93-5471-510-5

A CIP catalogue record for this book is available from the British Library.

Printed in India at Polykam offset New Delhi 110028

2 4 6 8 10 9 7 5 3 1

www.scholastic.co.uk

BE YOU
BOLD & BRILLIANT
JOURNAL

Introduction

Life is going to happen to you whether you decide to take control or not, but living the life you want isn't about what you are given.

Living the life you want is about **making smart choices**, **working really hard** and having **a lot of fun** along the way.

This journal is here to help you do just that! Complete the fill-in activities and quizzes, and use it to jot down your thoughts and keep track of your goals.

Let's get started!

Getting ORGANIZED

Life is all about making choices and decisions that will help you grow. You can start to do this by creating a list of things you want to focus on. Remember, life isn't a race, so pace yourself!

What I Will Work On:

never taking feeling good or happy for granted .... ☐

saying 'yes' to life's opportunities .... ☐

forgiving myself when I mess up .... ☐

standing up for what I believe in .... ☐

remembering that how I feel right now isn't how I'll feel for ever .... ☐

surrounding myself with good friends .... ☐

being kind whenever I have the opportunity .... ☐

making time for things that are important to me .... ☐

believing that I can achieve anything .... ☐

Procrastination

(the action of delaying or postponing something)

Ever put off doing things until later? Stay alert for **procrastination** and remember the sooner you finish your project, the sooner you can get back to doing what you want without feeling guilty about it!

Write down some of the tasks you'd like to complete in the shapes below.

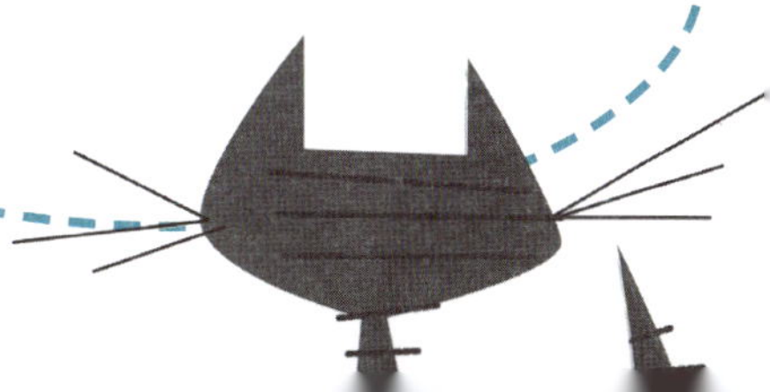

Let's Get Organized!

Do you ever have so much to do that it really stresses you out? Have a think about projects you'd like to tackle, and then put them in order of importance with 1 being **most** important and 10 being **least** important.

1. ....

....

2. ....

....

3. ....

....

4. ....

....

5. ....

....

6. ....

....

7. ....

....

8. ....

....

9. ....

....

10. ....

....

....

....

Take the Plunge: Revealing Quiz

Are you leading the life you want? Do you feel envious of people's lives around you? Well then, let's do something about it. Find out how you feel about your life with these six quick questions.

1. You hear that your school is having auditions for the play and you'd love to get a part in it. You…

a. Put your name on the list right away. This could be the start of your fabulous acting career.
b. Decide to wait until next time. You are already busy and don't want to overstretch yourself.
c. Don't bother. They always pick the same people so there is no point signing up.

2. You are on holiday and they have a kids' club at the resort. The kids in the club seem to be having a great time. You…

a. Ask your parents if you can join them. You have always wanted to try waterskiing.
b. Think about it. Maybe tomorrow, you've just started your magazine.
c. Stay well away. There's no way it will be as fun as it looks and what if no one talks to you?

3. You have a big test next week and you want to get a good mark. You…

a. Get studying!
b. Feel nervous so you spend all of your time making a beautiful study timetable.
c. It's hard and boring so you check if your favourite TV show is on to take your mind off it.

4. Your teacher says that the student with the best animal project will get the chance to help out at the local vets for the day. You love animals so you…

a. Put 100 per cent into your project. This is just your thing.
b. Imagine how much fun you'll have with the animals and not leave enough time for your project.
c. Do your project but try not to get too excited. There is no way it will be you.

5. A new girl starts at your school and your teacher asks for a volunteer to show her around. You…

a. Put your hand up – you are happy to help.
b. Wait to see if anyone else volunteers. You'd prefer to get to know her in your own time.
c. Keep your hands in your pockets and avoid eye contact with your teacher.

6. Your mum says that you can have a birthday party and invite anyone you like. You…

a. Immediately invite your whole class, your swimming club, the chess club and the school magazine. This is going to be the best party ever!
b. Plan an awesome party in your head but send the invites too late.
c. Only invite your best friend over for a sleepover. What if you invite other people and they don't come?

Conclusion

Mostly As – in at the deep end
You are always the first to sign up for everything. You love life and want to get as much out of it as possible. Make sure you don't take on too much though, you don't want to tire and stress yourself out.

Mostly Bs – paddling in the shallow end
You have big dreams and can't wait to start living them … tomorrow. It is a good idea to think before you leap, but make sure your chances don't pass you by. Life is short, so get organized, get involved and start having fun!

Mostly Cs – still in the changing room
It's not that you don't have ambitions, it's just that you get nervous and don't want to be disappointed. Try to put your nerves to one side, put on your favourite outfit, pretend you are feeling confident and get out there.

Overcoming Fear

Everyone gets scared – it's part of what makes us human! But that shouldn't stop you from trying new things or trying to overcome your fears. **Identify** some of your fears and **brainstorm** ways to overcome them.

My fear: presenting in front of a large group

How I can overcome this fear: by practising speaking in front of smaller groups, maybe even just a few friends to help grow my confidence.

My fear: ....

....

How I can overcome this fear: ....

....

My fear: ....

....

How I can overcome this fear: ....

....

My fear: ....

....

How I can overcome this fear: ....

....

My fear: ....

....

How I can overcome this fear: ....

....

Do you get scared of trying new things? Well don't let that stop you – a lot of scary things can be exciting. Often, it can help to simply **imagine** yourself succeeding! Even if doesn't go well… at least you'll have a funny story to tell afterwards.

The Sky is the Limit!

Make a conscious effort to **try new things** – this'll help you grow as an individual and you might even discover a new favourite hobby! Use this section to plan all the new things you want to try.

Motivation

Motivation comes in many forms – whether you're rewarding yourself with a treat after completing a difficult task you've been putting off, or listening to your favourite music as you study.

Motivational mantras and inspiring quotes can also help provide a quick burst of motivation.

Use this space to jot down your favourite motivational quotes, or even make up your own!

1. ....

....

....

2. ....

....

....

3. ....

....

....

4. ....

....

....

Classroom 1

School LIFE

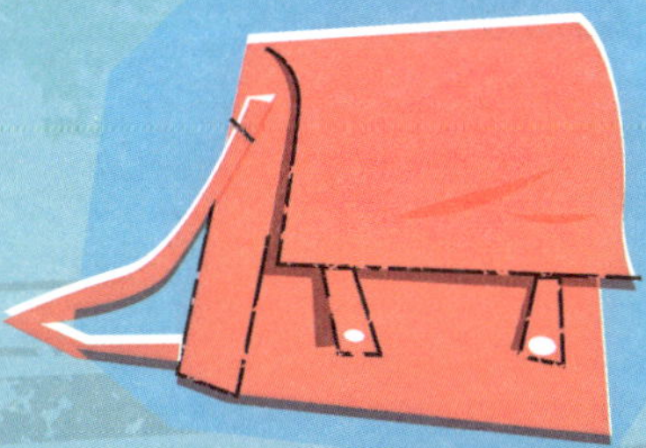

Learning to speak 'Teacher'

Ever feel like your teacher is speaking gibberish? Sometimes it can even seem like teachers have their own language! See if you can match these phrases from the mysterious language of 'teacher-speak' to what they might actually mean! Answers are at the bottom of the opposite page.

1\. 'See me'

2\. 'Could do better'

3\. 'There are no stupid questions'

4\. 'There are no wrong answers'

A. Your teacher sees great things in you and wants to see you achieve them. If you're struggling, why not ask them to give you a few pointers. They will be pleased to see you making the effort.

B. When a teacher says this, they want you to think creatively and be brave. So what if you say something silly – you never know, things might just get interesting ... for a change.

C. Your teacher wants you to feel like you can ask them anything, but do try to stay on topic!

D. It can be scary when you see this – especially if it's written in red pen on your homework, but don't panic! Teachers have A LOT of books to mark and don't have time to write an explanation on everyone's work. They probably just want to help you understand something a bit better.

Answers: **1D; 2A; 3C; 4B**

Things that make ME a good student

1. ....

....

....

2. ....

....

....

3. ....

....

....

4. ....

....

....

5. ....

....

....

Things that I could do to be a BETTER student

1. ....

2. ....

3. ....

4. ....

5. ....

Top Tips on How to DE-STRESS

Sometimes school stress can be overwhelming. Between homework, chores, after-school clubs and trying to fit in as much TV time as possible, there just aren't enough hours in the day! Eliminate school stress and get organized with these worry-busting tips.

GET UP!

If you struggle to get up in the morning, **set your alarm one hour before you need to leave the house**. This will give you plenty of time to snooze, wash, dress, have breakfast and double check that you have everything you need.

GET IN!

Unpack your school bag and change into your house clothes as soon as you get in. Give your parents any notes from school and anything that needs washing. You will be able to **de-stress much quicker** if you know this is taken care of.

GET ORGANIZED!

If you know you've got after-school club on Monday, it's the next episode of your favourite show on Wednesday and you're going away for the whole weekend, then **don't procrastinate**. Get your homework done on Tuesday and Thursday for a stress-free week. Simple!

GET IT DONE!

Make a space to do your homework and get it done ASAP. This will give you the rest of the night off and **stop that 9 o'clock panic** when you remember the homework you haven't done. When you've finished, put it straight back in your bag so you don't forget it in the morning.

GET TO BED!

Pack your school bag before you go to bed. Make sure you have your homework, your PE kit (if you need it) and any notes that you needed your parents to sign. You will **sleep much better knowing that you are prepared** for the next day. Sleep is also an excellent stress buster and improves your memory, so make sure you are getting enough: about 10 hours a night.

Though the tips on the previous pages are sure to help you de-stress, everyone is different and so each individual has different worries. What do you think could help YOU de-stress?

When I'm feeling stressed I...

Use this page to doodle, scribble or write down your thoughts.

'I attribute my success to this: I never gave or took any excuse.'

FLORENCE NIGHTINGALE

Q. I didn't finish my maths homework last week because it was really hard. I spent hours on it but still got in trouble. We get maths homework every week, it's so unfair! What should I do?

A. Unfortunately, you can't get out of maths homework, but you can make this situation easier. Speak to your teacher. Show them your homework after class and tell them how long you spent on it. Explain which bits you found hard. Don't be embarrassed – you are at school to learn and it's smart to ask for help. Honestly, it'll make things easier in the long run.

Q. I am frightened of the big kids at my new school. At my last school, I was in one of the oldest classes and I knew everyone. What should I do?

A. Moving from being a big fish in a little pond to being a tiny fish in an enormous ocean can feel really scary. Try joining a lunchtime or after-school club that has students from different years. As soon as you get to know some of the big kids, you'll see that they are just like you, but bigger, and not so scary after all.

Q. For the next class project I'm in a group with some classmates I don't know very well and all my friends are together. I feel left out and sad. Should I ask to switch?

A. You could ask to switch, but don't be surprised if your teacher refuses. Use this opportunity to get to know some other people in your class a bit better. You might find you work better without your best buds to chat to. This project won't last for ever and your friends will be sure to fill you in on anything you missed out on.

Q. I hate school. I dread going so much that I feel sick every morning. My teacher is nice and I have friends but I hate going. How can I persuade my mum to stop making me go?

A. You might have 'school phobia', where a person is so scared of going to school that they have real physical symptoms, like feeling and being sick, headaches and sleeplessness. Talk to a grown-up you trust about how you feel. They can make an appointment at school to discuss what it is you are scared of and what can be done to make it easier for you. The most important thing is that you speak to someone about it. The sooner you speak to someone, the sooner you can start feeling better.

Q. I am being teased at school because I get good marks and put my hand up to answer questions. I like school but I don't like getting picked on. What should I do?

A. You're a hard-working person that's going places, but it can be difficult to remember that when you are being called names. Whatever you do, don't dumb yourself down. Some people find schoolwork hard and, rather than studying, they like to tease others to distract from themselves. Don't take it to heart – it often isn't personal – and don't change who you are because of it.

You spend a large chunk of your life in school. It makes up a **large part of your daily life** so it sucks when you aren't enjoying it. But you're not alone!

Here are some people who didn't have the best time in school but are **super successful** now. You might even recognize some of them!

But school can have its perks! Here are five reasons why school rocks:

1. Friends

It might not be your first choice of venue, but at least you get to see your friends and catch up on the latest gossip.

2. Lunch

The food may be awful, but a whole hour to hang out with your favourite pals is the best.

3. PE

So, running up and down the school hall – also known as the 'bleep test' – can be hilarious if you are with the right people and at least it's not assembly ... right?

4. After-school clubs

Whether it's drama club, book club or running and track, there are so many fun things to choose from. Try something new, you might discover a hidden talent!

5. Holidays

Christmas, Easter, half-term ... the summer ... ahhh! You are rarely more than six weeks away from your next break. Smile – the term will be over before you know it.

My favourite after-school club is...

My favourite hangout spot is...

I like spending my free time with...

My favourite music to listen to is...

Draw your favourite lunch below:

My favourite subject is...

because:

A HEALTHY, Happy You

'Be healthy – and take care of yourself – but be happy with the beautiful things that make you, you.'

BEYONCÉ

GET MORE THAN Five a Day

You've probably heard how you are supposed to try to eat five pieces of fruit or veg a day, but did you know that some experts believe that you should **eat EIGHT a day**?

DRINK ONE

Have a glass of fruit or vegetable juice to kick-start your day. Don't drink too much though – it's full of sugar and doesn't contain the fibre.

START EARLY

Eat some fruit for breakfast. Sprinkle some blueberries or raspberries on to your cereal or try sliced apple with your toast.

SNACK SMART

Swap snacks for fruit. A fresh ripe nectarine or plum will keep your hunger pangs at bay much longer than a chocolate bar or bag of crisps.

SNEAK THEM IN

Add peas or sweetcorn to your pasta sauce and add another vegetable to your evening meal. Meat and two veg? Make it meat and three.

KEEP IT INTERESTING

Experiment with different, new and exciting fruit and vegetables. Look out for exotic treats at the supermarket like kiwi fruit or dragon fruit.

HAVE DESSERT

Chop up fresh fruit and serve with a dollop of Greek yoghurt and chopped nuts. #Yum!

Which fruit and veggies do you like and which can you not stand? Draw or write your likes and dislikes below!

What's on Your Plate?

There is no such thing as **bad food**, it's just all about moderation. Check out the **too-good-to-be-true** plate below to see how you **should** be eating each day. Try keeping these ratios in mind when you are choosing your lunch.

Fruit and vegetables
Make sure you are getting at least your five a day, if not eight.

Wholegrains and potatoes
Switch from white to wholegrain bread and pasta whenever possible. It's packed with heart-healthy fibre.

Dairy
Milk, yoghurt and cheese. Full of protein and calcium to keep your growing bones strong. Non-dairy alternatives include almond milk, nuts, green veggies and soy.

Non-nutritional treats
You can have your favourite sugary drinks and sweets or anything very high in fat, like chips or doughnuts – just in moderation. Make sure that they don't make up too much of what you eat each day and enjoy the treat.

Non-dairy protein
Lean meat, fish, beans. Proteins are the building blocks of every cell in your body so it makes sense that you need to eat some regularly.

Exercise Wise

#GetMoving

Keeping active is good for your physical and mental health. You are always on the go, whether it's running for the bus or during PE. But if you find exercise boring, try some of the tips below to help you liven it up.

GET PERSONAL

Just because you don't like sport doesn't mean you don't like exercise. Maybe the whole 'competitive thing' turns you cold. Come up with your own exercise programme and try to do it three times each week.

GET FUNKY

Put on your favourite music and dance around your room. This is great exercise, as it will get your heart pumping in no time.

GET BENDY

Yoga is an awesome way to exercise. It helps improve your posture and flexibility, reduces stress and can help you to sleep better. You can find a class near you or even find some basic Yoga videos online.

GET YOUR SKATES ON

Rollerblading is great exercise, take a pair to the park and get your heart racing. Don't forget your helmet and safety pads!

GET EVERYBODY MOVING

You will be much more likely to want to exercise if you do it with someone you enjoy spending time with. Why not go for a walk with your family or friends? You can even have a good goss as you go.

Mirror, Mirror

Do you like what you see when you look in the mirror? If the answer is no, stop right there. Magazines and adverts can make you believe that there is only one way to look and one definition of beauty, when that is absolutely not true. They stop you from seeing how **amazing** you are. Loving yourself can be hard but making it a priority can make a real difference. Here are some top tips to loving yourself. #NoFilter

You are unique – stop focusing on what you THINK is wrong with your body and think about all the amazing things it is able to do. Loving your body will help you to treat it with the love and respect it deserves.

Be kind to yourself – ever tell yourself that you're a loser, with weird hair and a big chin? If you heard a person talking about someone else that way, you would think they were very rude, so stop talking to yourself that way.

Take five – fight negative feelings by finding at least five things that make you fabulous. #LoveYourself

Be kind to others – do you flick through magazines and say mean things about celebs? Stop! Seeing the positive in others will help you to look for it in yourself.

Take responsibility – people can tell you that you are pretty, but until you start telling yourself that, you won't believe them. Don't brush off their compliments – be polite and say 'thank you'.

Get comfortable – being confident in your own skin makes other people want to be around you. Love yourself and others will follow.

We all have flaws – even the most beautiful people think they have flaws. After all, nobody is perfect. The key is to keep it in perspective. If you find yourself feeling unhappy and behaving differently because of how you look, talk to an adult you trust.

Words I would use to describe ME

Add your photo/draw a picture of yourself here

Words my family and friends would use to describe ME

'I've learned that people will forget what you said, people will forget what you did, but people will <u>never</u> forget how you made them feel.'

MAYA ANGELOU

TAKING CARE OF YOUR Mental Health

Keeping physically active is vital but sometimes we forget that managing our mental health is just as important! Everyday life – juggling school and friends and family and everything else! – can get a bit much.

Make sure to take breaks and focus on yourself. Don't know where to start? Check out our self-care top tips!

TOP SELF-CARE TIPS

Play for fun

Not everything has to be a competition! Whether it's a videogame or a sport, remember to enjoy yourself.

You are full of potential

Don't feel bad if you're not at a point in your life where you can look back and feel proud of your accomplishments yet. You are full of potential!

Keep a diary or journal

Writing about your day will help you identify how you are feeling and give you a record of how you felt in the past. Sometimes things that made you feel really sad a few weeks ago can seem silly when you look back at them.

Talk to someone you trust

Okay, so a problem shared isn't always a problem halved. I mean, who would be able to work that out accurately anyway? But talking about a problem will give you another person's point of view and they can help you work out what it is that is making you feel a certain way. Don't struggle with your feelings alone.

Listen to others

Listening to other people talk about how they feel not only gives you the opportunity to be a good friend, but also helps you to keep your own problems in perspective. Seeing how someone else handles their feelings and problems can help you learn a lot about how to handle your own.

BEWARE!

If you find that listening to a particular friend leaves you feeling more unhappy, beware – there's nothing misery loves more than company. Be a good friend to them, but make sure you surround yourself with friends who leave you feeling positive too.

'The battles that count aren't the ones for gold medals. The struggles within yourself – the invisible, inevitable battles inside all of us – that's where it's at.'

JESSE OWENS

Hobbies are a great way to build skills, make friends or just have fun – and they can improve your mental health and wellbeing. Here are a few hobbies you could try!

Join a debate club

Try yoga

Try rollerblading

Other hobbies I'd like to try: ....

....

....

Take swimming lessons

DIFFICULT Feelings

There are no such things as **good feelings** or **bad feelings**. All feelings are natural, even though some of them make us feel dreadful. When you feel something difficult, like anger or stress, it is the same as when you feel pain, it means that there is something amiss. Read on for a few tips on how to deal with some of life's more difficult feelings.

Anger

There is nothing wrong with being angry, it can even be good to help motivate you to do better. But the problem with anger is when you don't recognize it, you lose control and may say nasty things or become violent.

ANGER can make you:

- **red faced and sweaty**
- **say horrible things**
- **cry**
- **violent**
- **get headaches and stomach aches.**

Try handling your anger before doing something you regret with these temper-taming tips:

- **breathe deeply and count to ten**
- **walk away**
- **exercise to burn off angry energy**
- **think of happy memories or something funny**
- **talk to someone**
- **sing at the top of your lungs.**

When you have calmed down, think about what it was that made you angry and why, and who you should speak to about it.

Sadness

Like anger, lots of things in life will make you sad – not getting picked for a team, losing something important to you, someone moving away, falling out with friends, even someone else being sad can make you feel blue. It is natural for some things to make you feel sad but be careful it doesn't take over all areas of your life.

SADNESS can make you:

- **clam up and not want to talk**
- **cry**
- **not want to get up in the morning**
- **stomp around grumpily**
- **angry**
- **misbehave.**

The next time you feel blue try some of these sadness-solving solutions:

- **talk to someone**
- **think positive and smile**
- **try not to dwell**
- **remember this feeling will pass**
- **treat yourself.**

Sadness is like a scab, sitting around and picking at it all day will only make it worse. Feeling positive and moving forward by treating yourself or being kind to others can make you feel much better.

Most sadness will pass pretty quickly, but if you start to feel sad more often than happy it is very important that you talk to an adult you trust. Don't struggle on your own.

Nerves

You are standing in front of the class about to read the essay you wrote and you freeze. Your hands feel sweaty, your stomach is churning, oh my goodness … you think you are going to cry. STOP!

Follow these four steps to handle and overcome NERVES!

1. Focus on something still, like the clock or a poster or someone's painting of a silly owl.

2. Breathe in slowly through your nose and breathe out even more slowly through your mouth, whistling VERY QUIETLY through your teeth. Focus on the whistle. It is almost impossible to cry and whistle at the same time.

3. As you breathe, imagine yourself being filled with warm, glowing confidence. Everyone wants you to do well – even the owl picture. You were born to do this.

4. What are you standing there, breathing and whistling for? GO! You've got this!

Embarrassment

#OhTheShame

You feel sweaty, flustered, your face is going red and you need to run far away! **EMBARRASSMENT** is sneaky and cannot be predicted or prevented. It can cause anger, sadness, stress and make your cheeks burn! What can you do?

1. Check if anyone has noticed. If they haven't, you might just get away with it. Fingers crossed.

2. Try not to get too hung up on what happened. Leave it in the past!

3. Laugh along if people tease you about it. If people think it bothers you they will bring it up even more.

4. Even if people are talking about it, remember that this too shall pass. It will be old news in no time.

5. Remember that what doesn't kill you, makes you interesting. Embarrassing moments make great stories.

Guilt trip

Ever done something so wrong that it left you feeling really horrible inside? Feeling guilty sucks, here's how to get through it and come out smiling on the other side.

GUILT can make you:

- **lose sleep and concentration**
- **cry**
- **feel really bad inside and judge yourself**
- **want to pretend as though you did nothing wrong.**

All this ickiness is hard work but it can be really good for you. Feeling guilty can also make you:

- **take responsibility**
- **do your best never to do it again**
- **remind you of how what you do affects others.**

Own up

Keeping guilt bottled up and not owning up will eat away at you. No matter how bad you think what you did was, you will feel better when you admit it and apologize. Even if you're not forgiven immediately, you've been honest and said 'sorry'.

Let it go

You did something, you felt bad, you said sorry – it's time to let it go. Constantly replaying the situation over and over is unhealthy. You've learnt from your mistake, so stop punishing yourself.

Fake guilt begone!

Ever felt guilty when you know for a fact that you didn't do anything wrong? Like when your friend did really badly on a test and you did really well? This won't help you or your friend – let it go! You can still celebrate your success while supporting your friend through their difficult time.

Stress

You will definitely have heard adults saying that they are stressed out, but what do they know about it … right? Between school, friendships, homework, annoying siblings, after-school commitments and more homework, it's hard to keep on top of it all and stay calm.

A little stress can be really helpful. Good stress can make you feel just the right amount of nervous to make you get something done but too much stress is a bad thing.

When STRESS gets out of control, it can make you:

- **easily distracted and forgetful**
- **cry**
- **grumpy**
- **scared**
- **sleep badly**
- **eat differently**
- **have headaches and even throw up.**

Follow these stress-stomping suggestions the next time you start to feel frazzled.

1. Write a list of what is stressing you out.

2. Take a deep breath and prioritise the important things.

3. Talk about it with someone you trust.

4. Get some rest – a good night's sleep can do wonders.

5. Eat plenty of fruit and veg rather than junk – and don't skip meals!

Good Grief

When you lose someone you love, the feeling of sadness that you experience is called grief.

GRIEF can make you:

- **angry with the person who died**
- **angry with people who aren't grieving the way you are**
- **angry with the people who haven't felt grief**
- **pretend that nothing has changed**
- **feel guilty about things you did or didn't say to the person who died**
- **lose sleep and not want to eat**
- **feel numb and empty**
- **cry a lot right away and later, over unexpected things**
- **feel guilty every time you laugh or feel happy.**

Grief is different for everyone

When you grieve you may feel all of these things or none. Grief is different for everyone and just because someone doesn't cry or seems to carry on as normal, it doesn't mean that their grief is any less real than yours. Grief is a natural and very important emotion, and although it can be horrible it is the first step to feeling better.

Learn to share

Talking about your feelings can make you feel less alone, but it can be difficult. When you lose someone, it can be really hard to talk about them, even though you think about them all the time. Sometimes people around you are also grieving and that can make you not want to talk about the person that died in case you upset them. Take it slowly and only talk when you feel comfortable. Recall happy memories – remembering can be painful, but it can be comforting too.

Time heals, but not completely

When you lose someone or something it will be the biggest thing in your life for a long time. Eventually though, other parts of life will start sneaking in. This can make you feel guilty, but it shouldn't – your life has to, and should, go on. Your grief will never fully go away, you will always carry a little piece of it, but it will get easier and easier to handle.

Things I Love

Use this section to jot down all the things that make you happy. This could be activities, food, or even your favourite people!

'I think you have to love yourself before you fall in love...

'I'm still learning to love myself.'

SERENA WILLIAMS

Future ME

Dear Future Self...

Imagine who you will be when you are 30 years old... What will you be doing? Who will you be friends with? Where will you work? Where will you live? Write a letter to your future self that you can look back at in years to come as a reminder of everything you've accomplished.

To

The Future's Bright …

AND THE FUTURE IS YOURS!

Thinking about the future can be scary… but it can also be really fun! Whether you know where you want to be in five or even ten years' time, or you're just going with the flow, there is no limit to what you can – and will – achieve.

Take a look at the list of jobs below. You never know, maybe they'll inspire you and you may just spot your dream job in the mix!

Dream job
Marine biologist

What to dream about
Studying tropical fish and dolphins. Helping to preserve and restore our coral reefs.

What you can do now
Borrow a book on tropical fish from your local library.
Join a local youth wildlife group.

Dream job
Actor

What to dream about
Playing Juliet at The Globe Theatre, London, or starring in an award-winning, hit TV series.

What you can do now
Audition for as many school performances as you can. Join a drama club or even set up your own. Practise in front of small groups of friends and family.

Dream job
Doctor or nurse

What to dream about
Taking care of people and saving lives at home or anywhere in the world.

What you can do now
Help take care of a family member the next time they are feeling unwell. Take a beginner's First Aid course.

Dream job
Journalist

What to dream about
Reporting the news from all around the world.

What you can do now
Watch the news. Look out for newsworthy stories around you and try to write about them in an exciting way. Join a drama group to give you confidence and a good presenting style. Practise writing daily.

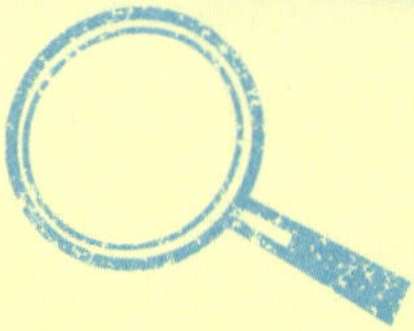

Dream job
Detective

What to dream about
Unravelling mysteries and fighting crime.

What you can do now
Do lots of puzzles. Tuning your mind to look for patterns and solving the unsolvable will be a good skill in the future.

Dream job
Writer

What to dream about
Writing stories to be enjoyed by readers all over the world from anywhere in the world!

What you can do now
Start writing now, even if it is just a diary. Try to write every day, even if it's just a little bit. Create characters and stories in your head. Read as much as you can, this can be a source of inspiration and can help improve your own writing.

Now that you've had a few examples, write about your own dream job below! It can be one of the examples given or something totally new.

MY DREAM JOB:

Wonder WOMEN

Having role models you can look up to can be an excellent source of motivation. A reminder that though no one is perfect, there are individuals who are living proof that you can become whoever you want to be, no matter who you are and where you come from.

Check out these real-life inspiring women who are breaking stereotypes and making a name for themselves.

'If you truly pour your heart into what you believe in, even if it makes you vulnerable, amazing things can and will happen.'

Emma Watson

Born: 1990

Then: grew up while starring in the mega-successful *Harry Potter* films and yet still managed to fit her schoolwork around filming and modelling. She achieved excellent grades in all of her exams. In 2014, she graduated Brown University, Rhode Island, USA, with a degree in English and was made UN Women Goodwill Ambassador in the same year!

Now: alongside her amazing acting career, Emma continues to be an advocate for women's rights and gender equality and has founded 'Our Shared Shelf' – an intersectional, feminist bi-monthly book club with thousands of participants.

'It doesn't matter who you are, where you come from. The ability to triumph begins with you. Always.'

Oprah Winfrey

Born: 1954

Then: as a girl, Oprah suffered abuse and faced bullying, racism and sexism. She worked hard and did well in school even though she had a very difficult home life. When she was 17, Oprah won a beauty pageant sponsored by a radio station that gave her a part-time job presenting the news.

Now: for 25 years, Oprah presented her very own mega-successful TV show, and became the world's first black, female billionaire. She owns her own TV channel, publishes her own magazine, founded a school for underprivileged girls in South Africa and donates millions of dollars to charities. She has even been nominated for an Oscar and, in 2013, was presented with the Presidential Medal of Freedom!

'It's hard when you feel down and you think, "Why is the world doing this to me?" But you have to pick yourself up again. That's what makes you a better athlete.'

Jessica Ennis-Hill

Born: 1986

Then: growing up, Jessica was the smallest in her class and was bullied by the bigger girls. She used to dread going to school and dreaded it even more when the same bullies followed her to secondary school. Instead of fighting, Jessica confided in her diary and eventually her mum. Her mum signed her up to an out-of-school sports camp where she began to compete.

Now: an Olympic champion and three-times world champion heptathlete, Jessica Ennis-Hill is considered one of Britain's most successful athletes! She received an MBE for her services to athletics in 2011 and later received a damehood in 2017. She also launched the 2020 Running World Cup alongside other athletes, including Usain Bolt.

'I raise up my voice – not so I can shout but so that those without a voice can be heard... We cannot succeed when half of us are held back.'

Malala Yousafzai

Born: 1997

Then: as a teenager, Malala spoke out and blogged on international news websites about girls' rights to education after girls in her hometown in Pakistan were banned from attending school. She overcame persecution for speaking out and, at 15 years old, survived being shot by the Taliban.

Now: Malala now lives in England and was a co-winner of the 2014 Nobel Peace Prize. She studied Philosophy, Politics and Economics at Oxford University and has published her own bestselling autobiography. She continues to speak at conventions all over the world, including at United Nations conferences.

Wonder Women WHO INSPIRE ME

Fill in this section with wonder women who inspire you! Draw or stick in their pictures.

Name:

....

What they do:

....

How they inspire me:

....

....

Name:

....

What they do:

....

How they inspire me:

....

....

Name:

....

What they do:

....

How they inspire me:

....

....

Name:

....

What they do:

....

How they inspire me:

....

....

Name:

....

What they do:

....

How they inspire me:

....

....

What are SHORT-TERM goals?

A short-term goal is something you hope to achieve soon or in the near future!

What are LONG-TERM goals?

A long-term goal is something that might take a longer time to achieve! Something you gradually work towards.

Setting yourself goals is one way of making sure you're doing everything you can to be the best version of you! Use the next two pages to write some goals and how you plan on achieving them, then – here's the tricky part – stick to them!

Goal #1

What I want to achieve: ....

....

Is this a **short-term** or **long-term** goal?

....

Three things I can do to help me achieve this:

1. ....

....

2. ....

....

3. ....

....

Goal #2

What I want to achieve: ....

....

Is this a **short-term** or **long-term** goal?

....

Three things I can do to help me achieve this:

1. ....

....

2. ....

....

3. ....

....

Goodbye and Good Luck!

Still here? Yay! You made it to the end. Nice work! Now that you've filled everything in, you can always come back and revisit your memories, notes and the **top tips** sprinkled throughout this journal.

We hope this journal continues to help you handle whatever life throws at you and is a reminder that even the worst feelings will pass.

The future is yours to create and remember…

BE BOLD, BE BRILLIANT, BE YOU!